W9-ABY-991

AMERICAN HISTORY BY DECADE

The
1920s

Titles in the American History by Decade series are:

AMERICAN HISTORY BY DECADE

The
1920s

Gregory T. Farshtey

KIDHAVEN
PRESS™

THOMSON
———— ★ ————
GALE ™

San Diego • Detroit • New York • San Francisco • Cleveland
New Haven, Conn. • Waterville, Maine • London • Munich

LIBRARY OF CONGRESS CATALOGING-IN-PUBLICATION DATA

Farshtey, Gregory T.
  The 1920s / by Gregory T. Farshtey.
    v. cm. — (American History by Decade)
Includes bibliographical references and index.
Summary: Discusses the 1920s including Prohibition, fashion, music, and the stock
market crash.
  ISBN 0-7377-1514-6 (alk. paper)
1. United States—History—1919–1933—Juvenile literature. 2. Nineteen twenties—Juvenile literature. [1. United States—History—1919–1933. 2. Nineteen
twenties.] I. Title: Nineteen twenties. II. Title. III. Series.
  E784.F37 2004
  973.91'5—dc21
                                       2003003556

Printed in the United States of America

Contents

The Roaring Twenties

Americans in the 1920s wanted a change. World War I had ended in 1918. Fifty thousand Americans had died in the war. Another two hundred thousand were wounded. The hard times caused by the war and the loss of so many people had left Americans feeling tired. Men and women longed for a simpler time. They wished for a better time, both for themselves and their nation.

The new decade brought **prosperity** for many. Businesses blossomed. Employment grew. The new automobile industry alone employed 5 million people. Full-page advertisements in major newspapers hailed business executives as the nation's heroes.

Life felt good to many Americans. They danced to new music and followed new fads and fashions. For many the decade seemed like an endless party, fueled by jazz and home-made alcohol.

Times were so good that no one could have guessed how the 1920s would come to a close. By the end of the decade, prosperity had turned to financial disaster. The nation headed into the worst economic crisis in its history. Over 16 million people lost their jobs. But until that point, the decade more than earned its nickname: the Roaring Twenties.

CHAPTER ONE

Prohibition

Prohibition was the name given to a law that banned the making, selling, or drinking of any alcoholic beverage. Congress passed the law in the belief that alcohol abuse was responsible for crime, poverty, divorce, and many other social problems. In the end the law proved impossible to enforce and in fact led to the rise of organized crime and a huge increase in alcohol abuse among Americans.

The idea of banning alcohol had been debated for years between supporters, nicknamed "drys," and those opposed, called "wets." The drys were able to get the law passed for a number of reasons. They were better organized than the wets, with a powerful political **lobby group**. Many of the wets were saloon owners or liquor manufacturers and so they did not have good reputations. In addition, many Americans were thinking about the nation's entry into World War I and simply were not paying attention. Protests against passage of the law were scattered and small.

America Goes Dry

On January 17, 1920, America officially went dry. The Eighteenth Amendment to the Constitution became the law of the land that day. The amendment made it a crime to "manufacture, sell, barter, transport, import, export, deliver, furnish or possess"[1] any alcoholic beverage. Prohibition would last for thirteen years.

A poster from the Prohibition era urges Americans to give up alcohol for the sake of women and children.

When the law was passed, its supporters saw it as the first step toward social reforms of all kinds. Without the temptation of liquor, they argued, men would spend more time with their families, work harder, go to church more regularly, and live cleaner lives. "The reign of tears is over," evangelist Billy Sunday said when Prohibition became law. "The slums will soon be a memory. We will turn our prisons into factories and our jails into storehouses and corncribs. Men will walk upright now, women will smile and the children will laugh."[2]

The hoped-for reforms did not take place. Most Americans had no interest in changing their drinking habits.

Most Americans, like the occupants of this car, did not want to give up alcohol.

On the day before the law went into effect, city streets all over the nation were crowded with people rushing bottles of liquor home in wagons, baby carriages, and anything else that had wheels. These would be the last legal purchases of alcoholic drinks for thirteen years, but the illegal trade in beer, wine, and hard liquor was about to explode.

Bootleggers

People wanted to drink alcohol even though it was illegal, and criminals saw ways to make money by making and selling liquor. Americans who wanted a drink during Prohibition had a number of choices.

One of the most popular was to go to a **speakeasy**. These were illegal saloons that popped up in cities and towns all over the nation. (Their name came from the fact that they were supposed to be secret, and you had to "speak easy," or talk softly, when you spoke about them.) Speakeasies ranged from fancy nightclubs to dark, dingy, and often dangerous bars. In New York City there was a speakeasy on almost every block. Detroit, which had fifteen hundred bars operating before Prohibition, had fifteen thousand speakeasies by 1925.

Most speakeasies were owned by gangsters, and the liquor was supplied by smugglers called **bootleggers**. Some bootleggers brought in liquor from Canada, Mexico, or the Bahamas. Others hijacked liquor shipments belonging to other gangs. Still others made their own liquor.

People who could not afford speakeasies found other ways of getting alcohol. Some drank products that had alcohol in them. Many of these were unsafe for humans to drink. Hair tonic, rubbing alcohol, and antifreeze were just some of the things people tried to drink. Many died from poisoning as a result.

Even in speakeasies, beverages sold as whiskey, Scotch, or gin were often poisonous. These drinks were made with **denatured alcohol**, a type of alcohol that contains chemicals

A man kneels next to a sign on the sidewalk pointing the way to a speakeasy.

that are unfit for drinking. Some bootleggers tried to remove the chemicals from the alcohol before they sold it, but others did not know how or did not care. In one year over fifty thousand Americans died from drinking poisonous liquor.

Bathtub Gin

One way to avoid someone else's bad liquor was to make liquor in your own home. Stills began to appear in cities and country areas in great numbers from 1920 on. These were used to heat a fermented mixture of rye, sugar, and other ingredients. Using this mixture a person could make a powerful whiskey. Other people mixed ingredients in their bathtubs to make gin (called bathtub gin), or even fermented raisin cakes into wine.

Not every bootlegger or smuggler was a professional criminal. Alcohol could legally be sold to pharmacists for use in medicine. Many pharmacists found they could make a bigger profit selling the alcohol on the side to people who wanted a drink. One of the earliest smugglers was a New York cab driver who drove his cab 350 miles to Canada, loaded it up with whiskey bottles, and drove it back.

Corrupt Police

Nearly everyone in America, including the police, knew the law was being broken regularly. Prohibition turned out to be a law that could not be enforced. One of the biggest reasons for that was **corruption** among the police. It was the job of the police to arrest bootleggers and shut down speakeasies. Many police ignored the law. Some politicians had said this would be a problem before the law was even passed. New York congressman Fiorello La Guardia said, "In order to enforce Prohibition, it will require a police force of 250,000 men and a force of 250,000 to police the police."[3]

The son of one speakeasy owner remembers, "Some of the best customers we had were cops. Sometimes they'd pay for their drinks but mostly we'd take care of them. . . . When we'd bring in barrels of beer, we'd give the beat cop a dollar a barrel if he was watching."[4]

The gangsters who ran speakeasies were quick to bribe police, and the police, who were poorly paid, were quick to accept. Some bootleggers spent half their profits on bribes. In return the police tipped them off about planned raids and

A police department liquor squad poses with cases of confiscated alcohol. Many police officers, however, ignored the Prohibition law.

ignored illegal activities. In Chicago, police even helped truck caravans of bootlegged liquor travel through the city!

Cities Run by Gangsters

Many people were needed to run a bootlegging operation, but the amount of money that could be made was huge. This led to the growth of organized crime. Hijackings, gang wars, bribery of politicians, and murders increased so much that some cities were practically run by gangsters. Criminals like Al Capone and "Lucky" Luciano rose to wealth and power due to the success of their bootlegging business. Those federal agents and police who were honest were too few in number to be able to combat the gangs.

Worse, as people saw the police and their political leaders ignoring lawlessness, they lost their respect for the law and the political system. Juries in some districts refused to convict bootleggers. People began to believe that some criminals were so powerful that they could never be brought to justice. That attitude helped organized crime grow, even after Prohibition was ended.

Prohibition was **repealed** in 1933, mainly for economic reasons. With so many people out of work because of the depression, less tax money was coming in to the states. By making liquor sales legal again and taxing them, hundreds of millions of dollars of tax money began pouring in.

"Lucky" Luciano ran a successful bootlegging business.

In the thirteen years it was the law, Prohibition changed people's attitudes toward the police, government, and the legal system. It also made the gangster a powerful and popular figure in the eyes of many people.

CHAPTER TWO

Fashion

Changing times are often seen in changing clothing styles. Nowhere is this better shown than in the fashions of the 1920s. Major shifts in the role of women in society helped spark a dramatic change in clothing and hairstyles.

The change in women's roles during the 1920s began with passage of the Nineteenth Amendment to the Constitution. This amendment gave American women the right to vote. At the same time more women were attending college and entering the workforce than ever before. Younger women, especially, did not see the need to stay tied to the traditions and styles of the past. They wanted their own unique look. The most famous example of this was the flapper.

The Flapper

Modern young women of the 1920s were known as flappers. Their name came from the habit of wearing ankle-high galoshes unbuttoned. When the ladies walked the galoshes flapped, and people started saying, "Here come the flappers."[5]

Flappers dressed to shock. Their mothers had worn long skirts, long-sleeved blouses with high lace collars, heavy cotton underwear, heavy black stockings, and ankle-binding boots. Flappers' dresses had hemlines above the knee and were often short-sleeved or sleeveless. Beads and bows became common additions to women's clothing. With shorter skirts, stockings became more important. In the past women had worn modest black cotton stockings designed

Flappers wore dresses with hemlines above the knee.

for warmth. Now flesh-colored stockings made of **rayon**, or "artificial silk," and designed to look attractive became more popular. Flappers usually wore their stockings rolled down beneath the knee.

Other major changes involved hairstyles and the use of makeup. Before the flapper era, women's hairstyles were long and full. The use of makeup was discouraged. Many people believed that only women of low morals wore cosmetics.

A woman checks her makeup in a compact mirror. Interest in cosmetics rose considerably during the 1920s.

As with clothing, flappers created their own hairstyle. Women trimmed their hair short so that their necks were bare, a style called "the bob." They even started going to barbershops for haircuts. Barbers used to cutting men's hair were more skilled at doing the short cuts women now wanted.

Makeup was in use more often as well, especially rouge (blush) and lipstick. The appeal of cosmetics spread quickly. Working women had more money of their own to spend, and they chose to spend some of it on makeup. Beauty shops appeared in almost every city and town. Author Aldous Huxley described the new interest in women's beauty products this way: "Soaps, skinfoods, lotions, hair preservers and hair-removers, powders, paints, pastes, pills that dissolve your fat from inside, bath salts that dissolve it from without, instruments for rubbing your fat away, foods that are guaranteed not to make you fat at all, machines that give you electric shocks, engines that massage and exercise your muscles . . . A face cost as much in upkeep as a Rolls Royce."[6]

The flapper look spread all over the nation, thanks in part to the drawings of cartoonist John Held Jr. Held's drawings showed young women with rolled-down stockings living it up at parties and driving in roadsters. His art was published in popular magazines like *Life* and *The New Yorker*. His work became the model for many young women. After a while they started dressing and acting like the fun-loving, high-living characters in his drawings.

Grave Concern

Not everyone liked the new look and the new attitude of the flapper, however. One newspaper editorial worried publicly about harm to the American way of life. It stated: "The situation causes grave concern on the part of all who have the ideals at heart of purity and home life and the stability of our American civilization."[7] Other newspaper cartoons poked

A print ad promotes a beauty powder. Many different beauty products appeared during the 1920s.

John Held Jr.'s drawings of flappers, like this one on the cover of *Judge* magazine, helped spread the flapper look across the nation.

fun at the effect short skirts had on onlookers, showing women causing auto accidents just by walking down the street. State legislatures even tried to pass laws banning the new styles. Utah, in 1921, considered a law that would make it a crime to wear skirts higher than three inches above the ankle. Violators would be fined or imprisoned.

The new styles at times disrupted family life as well. One woman remembered her sister, who was a flapper, this way: "She wore beautiful short dresses, fur coats . . . hats that covered her head like a turban, and—of course—galoshes, always unbuckled. The day my sister came home with bobbed hair, my mother took one look at her and retired to the couch with her . . . smelling salts that kept her from fainting."[8]

Flappers wore hats and short hairstyles that shocked their families.

The Rise of Ready-to-Wear

The flapper look lasted through much of the decade. Toward the close of the 1920s, however, a new fashion trend began to appear. Called **ready-to-wear**, it consisted of suits and dresses made in factories and shipped in large numbers to

Near the end of the 1920s, mass-produced clothing became available in department stores.

Quelques modèles habillés.

Les Grandes Modes de Paris.
Supplément au Nº 366.

18, avenue de l'Opéra
PARIS

department stores. Ready-to-wear garments could be just as stylish as clothing that was made to order for a customer. But the ability to mass-produce clothing resulted in ready-to-wear being far less expensive than what one would get at a dressmaker's shop.

Although customers enjoyed the benefits of ready-to-wear clothing, tailors and dressmakers suffered. Their business slowed down a lot. One fashion survey in 1928 noted, "Women's garments are now for the first time being made in bulk by factory methods. Very soon it seems as if only the most exclusive men's and women's garments will be made by hand, so that dressmaking and tailoring will be purely luxury trades."[9]

The Fashion Legacy of the 1920s

Fashion in the 1920s was shocking, daring, and—finally—mass-produced. The decade changed the way styles became popular. After the 1920s fashion trends would be dictated more often by what young men and women chose to wear. The ready-to-wear system meant that new styles would not be seen only in big cities. They would be available in towns all around the nation, giving many more people the chance to dress in fashion.

CHAPTER THREE

The Jazz Age

T he 1920s are known as the Jazz Age. It was during this time that the new style of music called jazz became popular around the country. Jazz musicians became well-known stars, and new dances inspired by the music became nationwide crazes.

Jazz combines elements of African American spirituals with ragtime. It has a beat that makes people want to dance, clap, or tap their feet. Sometimes it seems to swing, other times it has a slow, soulful sound. One feature of jazz is that much of the music is made up on the spot. Jazz musicians use a melody as a starting point and then improvise, which means playing whatever notes feel right to them. The result was a rhythmic sound like nothing ever heard before.

Jazz Greats

The explosion in popularity of jazz took place mostly in the crowded cities of the north. The many nightclubs and speakeasies found in big cities such as Chicago and New York needed musical entertainment for their customers. The gangsters who owned the clubs had plenty of money to pay musicians. A jazz musician in Chicago, for example, could earn as much as $40 a session. The same musician in New Orleans at that time would earn $1.50 to $2 for the same work.

The club owners also found plenty of talent in the black musicians who had left the south and moved north to look for work. The best known was Louis Armstrong, a cornet and trumpet player who got his start playing with King Oliver's Creole Jazz Band. Armstrong was famous for his exciting style of trumpet playing, his gravelly voice, and his sense of humor. People respected his talent and liked his personality.

Jazz legend Louis Armstrong sits at a piano surrounded by his band, the Hot Five.

Armstrong quickly rose to stardom. Many jazz bands developed a following, but Armstrong drew crowds like no band ever could. In the mostly black neighborhoods of Harlem, young men began dressing like Armstrong. They even carried handkerchiefs in their hands everywhere as he did. One fan remembers driving around on a rainy night with his friends, sticking their heads out the window in hopes that their voices would turn hoarse and sound like Armstrong's.

Another popular jazz musician was Duke Ellington. He led a jazz orchestra and was also a talented composer. Ellington chose parts of many different American and European musical styles and made them into a single style. His time as the bandleader at New York's most famous jazz club, the Cotton Club, made him a star in that city. Radio broadcasts of his orchestra's performances made Ellington a household name around the nation.

Black, White, and Tan

Although Ellington became one of the most famous black jazz musicians by playing at the Cotton Club, the club itself did not let in black customers. Blacks and whites rarely mixed in the 1920s. They lived in separate parts of town, shopped at different stores, and attended different schools.

So, the Cotton Club's jungle decor was mostly designed for the benefit of whites. Many whites went to Harlem looking for a way to experience black culture. One performer remembers: "At the Cotton Club, the whites from downtown could see a show right in the middle of Harlem with the cream of black entertainment . . . and not have to be bothered rubbing elbows with the people who actually lived in the community." [10]

In other places jazz actually brought the races together. Chicago's "black and tan" clubs admitted both blacks and

Although the Cotton Club featured black musicians, only white customers were allowed.

whites to listen and dance to jazz music. These clubs were among the very few places in Chicago where blacks and whites mixed in this era.

The popularity of jazz also increased with the growth of the recording industry. Jazz records like Louis Armstrong's

"West End Blues," Jelly Roll Morton's "Original Jelly-Roll-Blues," and Duke Ellington's "East St. Louis Toodle-O" made it possible for people to hear top jazz artists without leaving their homes. Record sales soared, with over 100 million sold in 1927 alone.

Records and radio helped to make jazz a nationwide craze. Even fans who lived far from big cities could still discover the music and dance to it.

The Dance Craze

Jazz was music meant to be danced to, and it helped to make dance clubs and ballrooms more popular. Long lines could be seen every night outside of places like Chicago's Midway Dancing Gardens. Almost all of the people waiting to pay their $1.00 admission fee were young, and they were there to dance to jazz. One musician recalls: "People didn't think anything about going a hundred and fifty to two hundred miles to dance back in those times."[11]

New dances swept the nation. The most popular was the Charleston. It required very fast and sometimes complicated steps, such as crossing the hands on the knees while the knees moved back and forth. The Charleston filtered into every aspect of American society—even restaurants. Some waiters and waitresses, for example, performed the Charleston while customers waited for their food.

Other popular dances included the black bottom and the Lindy Hop. Both of these were high-energy, fast dances. A slower dance, the fox-trot, required partners to dance cheek to cheek. This shocked many people because few dances at this time involved physical contact.

Learning the steps to many of the dances took some effort. They were not always easy to master. Skilled dancers at places like the Savoy Ballroom in New York would often wear pieces of paper taped to their backs with phone numbers

Two women dance the Charleston on a rooftop. The Charleston was immensely popular across the nation.

The fox-trot, a popular slow dance, required couples to dance cheek to cheek.

or a studio name written on it. If another customer admired their dancing, they could contact the dancer to take lessons.

People who lived far from hot jazz spots, like the Cotton Club and the Apollo Theater, or dance halls like the Savoy Ballroom did not miss out on the new music. With record players and records, people could hear jazz and dance to it

In a depiction on the cover of the popular magazine *Judge*, a woman plays music on a record player. Record players helped spread the popularity of jazz music across the nation.

just about anywhere. Jazz dance parties livened up the night anywhere from private homes to college dormitories.

Another fad that grew out of jazz dancing was the dance marathon. Dancers would compete against each other to see who could keep dancing the longest. The prize was usually money. These contests were physically exhausting for the dancers. Most marathons lasted about a week. The longest on record went on for three weeks.

The Legacy of Jazz

Before the 1920s ended, jazz had won over Americans all across the country. Its appealing sound brought enjoyment to millions, and it influenced other forms of music in the years to come.

CHAPTER FOUR

The Stock Market Crash

Over the course of six days in October 1929, the U.S. **stock market** collapsed. After a decade of prosperity, many Americans suddenly found their savings wiped out. The stock market crash was the first giant step toward the Great Depression of the 1930s.

No single cause has ever been named for the Crash of 1929. But its effects were felt by rich and poor. It would be more than a decade before the American economy recovered.

Boom and Bust

The stock market was thought of as the fastest and easiest way to get rich in the 1920s. While only a small number of Americans invested in the stock market, it seemed like everyone knew someone who knew someone who had struck it rich. One employee of a **stockbroker** remembers: "Stock prices had been going up pretty steadily, and even though it was still mainly rich people investing, the average guy was starting to hear about friends making $20,000 or $30,000 overnight." [12]

Most people bought stocks by paying a small amount in a down payment. They borrowed the rest from the stockbroker who sold them the stock.

When stock prices suddenly began to fall on October 24, investors panicked. *The New York Times* described the scene

Then and Now

	1920	2000
U.S. population:	106,521,537	281,421,906
Life expectancy:	Female: 54.6 Male: 53.6	Female: 79.5 Male: 74.1
Average yearly salary:	$1,236	$35,305
Unemployment rate:	5.2%	5%

Source: Kingwood College Library.

on Wall Street in New York City, headquarters of the Stock Exchange: "Wall Street was a street of vanished hopes . . . and of a sort of paralyzed hypnosis yesterday. Men and women crowded the brokerage offices . . . Little groups gathered here and there to discuss the falling prices in hushed and awed tones."[13]

Nothing like this had happened in America before. By October 29 more than $25 billion in personal wealth had been lost. That day is known as Black Tuesday because of how

An artist depicts stockbrokers panicking on Wall Street as the
market crashes in 1929.

quickly and sharply stock values dropped. Sidney Weinberg, a senior stockbroker at the time, remembers the feeling on that day: "I stayed in the office a week without going home . . . It must have been ten or eleven o'clock before we got the final reports. It was like a thunder clap. Everyone was stunned. Nobody knew what it was all about."[14]

Losses Pile Up

When stock prices fell brokers demanded money from customers to cover their loans. Investors had to come up with cash or lose their stocks. People emptied their bank accounts in an effort to pay off their loans and keep their stocks. Comedian Groucho Marx had his entire life savings invested in the market and had to give his broker all the cash he had to keep his stocks from being sold. Later he wrote: "Some of the people I know lost millions. I was luckier. All I lost was $240,000. I would have lost more, but that was all the money I had."[15]

Men and women who had been rich on October 23 found themselves deeply in debt a week later. One man, for example, had a company worth $17 million in mid-October. By October 29 his company's value had dropped to nothing and he owed $3 million to three different banks.

Almost no one escaped the effects of the crash. I.W. Burnham was a college student in 1929, with the typical concerns of a student at that time. At first he did not understand how much impact the crash would have on him and his family: "I first heard about the crash when [my father] called me at school about it . . . Well, I was in college and I didn't realize how serious it all was. I mean, at that time in my life, the most important thing imaginable was buying a raccoon coat . . . So even after my father told me about the crash, I begged and pestered him to buy me that coat. Finally he gave it to me and said, 'Well, now you've got the coat, but we're

The front page of the newspaper *Variety* announces the stock market crash.

broke. I got wiped out in the market.' He had lost $200,000, which was everything we had. That's when I realized how bad it was."[16]

Effects of the Crash

Rumors spread of investors and stockbrokers by the dozens committing suicide. Though the rumors proved untrue, many people came close. The suffering that resulted from the crash was real and very painful. One investor remembers: "I don't know anybody that jumped out a window. But I know many who threatened to jump. They ended up in nursing

Men stand in line for food. Many people lost their jobs after the stock market crash.

homes and insane asylums and things like that . . . They broke down physically, as well as financially."[17]

The damage done by the crash to investors' bank accounts was easy to see. The full impact of the disaster took time to show itself. People who once had a lot of money stopped buying cars, boats, and other luxury items. They cut down on travel and stayed away from expensive hotels. Little by little the drop in business affected other businesses. After a while many companies around the country were suffering. Some lost so much business that they had to close. Others laid off workers because they could not pay them.

Unemployment rose. People who had once had good jobs could not find work. They did what they could to survive. Clara Hancox was eleven years old at the time of the crash and remembers seeing former businessmen on the streets of New York trying to earn a living peddling apples. "Respectable businesspeople would walk around in the streets of downtown Manhattan with a tray of bright red apples, and they would ask you to buy an apple for five cents. And horrible as that was, it was even more horrible that we didn't even have five cents!"[18]

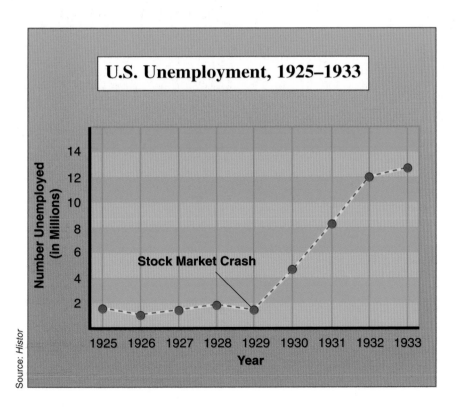

Source: *Histor*

As 1929 drew to a close, the effects of the crash were only beginning to be felt. The coming years would see its impact spread from one end of the nation to the other.

End of the Decade

The 1920s had begun with hope. The country was at peace; the economy was strong. People wanted to drink and dance and have fun. The crash brought the decade-long party to a sudden halt. As 1929 ended people looked back and wondered how everything had changed so rapidly. They also looked ahead with worry, wondering what the 1930s would bring.

Notes

Chapter One: Prohibition

1. Quoted in John Kobler, *Ardent Spirits: The Rise and Fall of Prohibition*. New York: GP Putnam's Sons, 1973, p. 215.
2. Quoted in Dennis Roddy, "The Constitution's 27 Amendments: The Way We Embrace Their Spirit Every Day," November 27, 2002. www.postgazette.com.
3. Quoted in John Kobler, *Ardent Spirits*, 1973, p. 223.
4. Quoted in Peter Jennings and Todd Brewster, *The Century*. New York: Doubleday, 1998, p. 122.

Chapter Two: Fashion

5. Quoted in *The Fainting Couch*, vol. 1, 2000. www.faintingcouch.com.
6. Quoted in Carolyn Hall, *The Twenties in Vogue*. New York: Harmony, 1983, pp. 13–14.
7. Quoted in Ezra Bowen, ed., *This Fabulous Century: 1920–1930*. New York: Time-Life Books, 1969, p. 30.
8. Quoted in Peter Jennings and Todd Brewster, *The Century*, p. 115.
9. Quoted in Elizabeth Ewing, *History of 20th Century Fashion*. Totowa, NJ: Barnes and Noble, 1986, p. 120.

Chapter Three: The Jazz Age

10. Quoted in Peter Jennings and Todd Brewster, *The Century*, p. 135.
11. Quoted in Geoffrey C. Ward and Ken Burns, *Jazz: A History of America's Music*. New York: Alfred A. Knopf, 2000, p. 124.

Chapter Four: The Stock Market Crash

12. Quoted in Peter Jennings and Todd Brewster, *The Century*, p. 142.

13. Quoted in Floyd Norris and Christine Bockelmann, *The New York Times Century of Business*. New York: McGraw-Hill, 2000, p. 81.

14. Quoted in Studs Terkel, *Hard Times: An Oral History of the Great Depression*. New York: Pantheon, 1970, p. 72.

15. Quoted in Karen Blumenthal, "Seeds of the 1929 Crash," November 2002. www.wsjclassroomedition.com.

16. Quoted in Peter Jennings and Todd Brewster, *The Century*, p. 142.

17. Quoted in Studs Terkel, *Hard Times*, p. 73.

18. Quoted in Peter Jennings and Todd Brewster, *The Century*, p. 150.

Glossary

bootlegger: Someone who makes, transports, and/or sells an illegal substance, usually alcohol.

corruption: Improper or illegal behavior such as taking bribes or selling favors.

denatured alcohol: Alcohol which has been treated so that it is unfit for drinking. This usually involves adding a toxic substance.

lobby group: An organization that attempts to get public officials to agree to an issue or set of issues.

prosperity: Financial success and well-being.

rayon: A manufactured fiber used in place of silk beginning in the 1920s.

ready-to-wear: Clothing made beforehand, usually in factories, for general sale.

repeal: To cancel or do away with a law.

speakeasy: A place where alcoholic beverages were illegally sold.

stockbroker: An agent who buys shares of stock in a company for another person with that person's money.

stock market: A place where securities (stocks) are bought and sold in an organized manner.

For Further Exploration

Books

Karen Blumenthal, *Six Days in October: The Stock Market Crash of 1929*. New York: Atheneum Books for Young Readers, 2002. Chronicles the six-day period in 1929 that shattered the American stock market, while explaining stock market fundamentals.

Stephen Feinstein, *The 1920s from Prohibition to Charles Lindbergh*. Berkeley Heights, NJ: Enslow, 2001. Looks at the history and lifestyle of the 1920s from the beginning of the decade to the start of the Great Depression.

Suzanne Lieurance, *The Prohibition Era in American History*. Berkeley Heights, NJ: Enslow, 2003. Traces the events of the thirteen years of Prohibition in the United States, with an emphasis on the people involved in significant events.

Websites

The Authentic History Center (www.authentichistory.com). Features a collection of images from the 1920s, as well as audio files related to the period.

PBS Online (www.pbs.org). Official site of the documentary film, "JAZZ: A Film by Ken Burns," features biographies, maps, articles, and classroom resources.

Vintagevixen.com (www.vintagevixen.com). "Sheiks and Shebas—Women's Fashions of the 1920s" offers an overview of the changes in women's fashions during the decade, and notable fads, with illustrations.

Index

Picture Credits

About the Author

Gregory T. Farshtey is an author of more than thirty books, including three novels, children's game books, and nonfiction. A graduate of the State University of New York at Geneseo, Farshtey is employed as a writer for a major children's magazine and website. He is usually writing, reading, or cooking Italian food at home in Rocky Hill, Connecticut.